CLASSICAL FAVORITES

15 TIMELESS MELODIES ARRANGED BY PHILLIP KEVEREN

— PIANO LEVEL —
ELEMENTARY

ISBN 978-1-5400-2834-1

Visit Hal Leonard Online at
www.halleonard.com

Visit Phillip at
www.phillipkeveren.com

Contact Us:
Hal Leonard
7777 West Bluemound Road
Milwaukee, WI 53213
Email: info@halleonard.com

In Europe contact:
Hal Leonard Europe Limited
Distribution Centre, Newmarket Road
Bury St Edmunds, Suffolk, IP33 3YB
Email: info@halleonardeurope.com

In Australia contact:
Hal Leonard Australia Pty. Ltd.
4 Lentara Court
Cheltenham, Victoria, 3192 Australia
Email: info@halleonard.com.au

PREFACE

The great melodies from the classical world provide the developing pianist with a wealth of great material. I would recommend seeking out a recording of each piece prior to studying the piano arrangement. Not only will you be inspired by what you hear, you will also get the "big picture" regarding phrasing, tempi, and style.

Sincerely,

Phillip Keveren

BIOGRAPHY

Phillip Keveren, a multi-talented keyboard artist and composer, has composed original works in a variety of genres from piano solo to symphonic orchestra. Mr. Keveren gives frequent concerts and workshops for teachers and their students in the United States, Canada, Europe, and Asia. Mr. Keveren holds a B.M. in composition from California State University Northridge and a M.M. in composition from the University of Southern California.

CONTENTS

ALSO SPRACH ZARATHUSTRA
(Thus Spoke Zarathustra)

By RICHARD STRAUSS
Arranged by Phillip Keveren

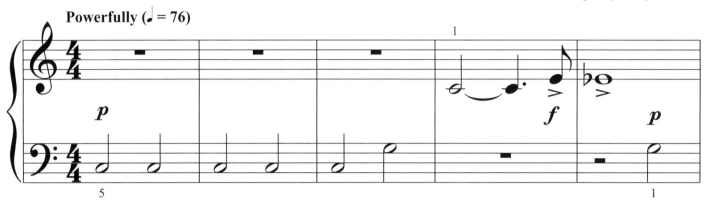

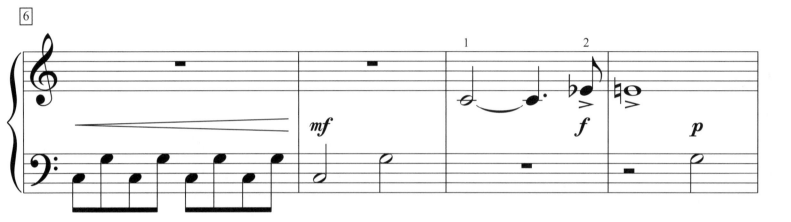

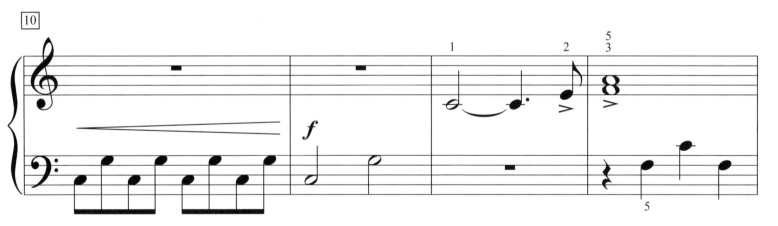

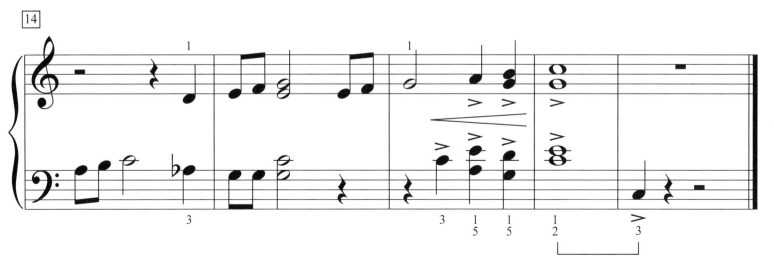

CANON IN D MAJOR

By JOHANN PACHELBEL

Arranged by Phillip Keveren

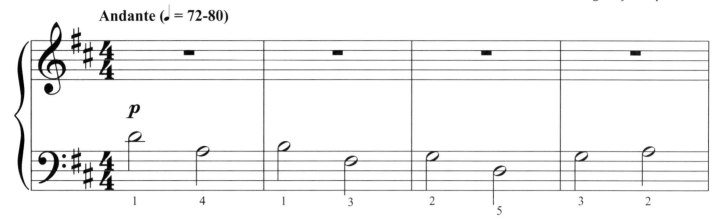

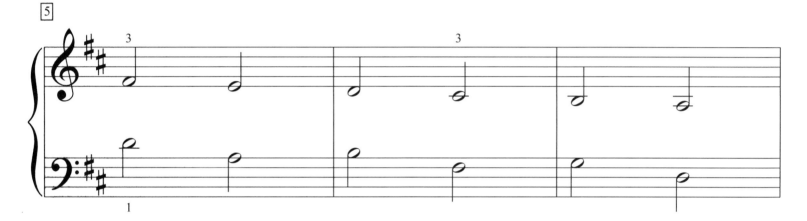

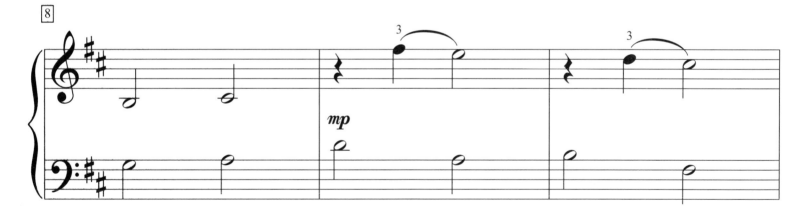

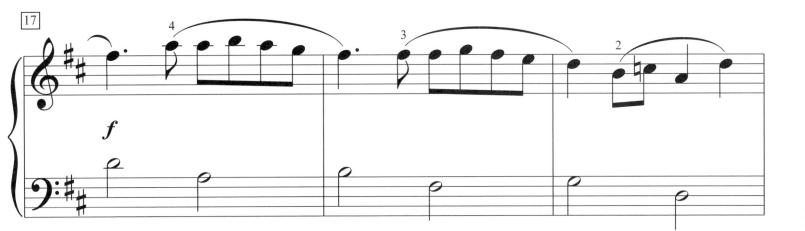

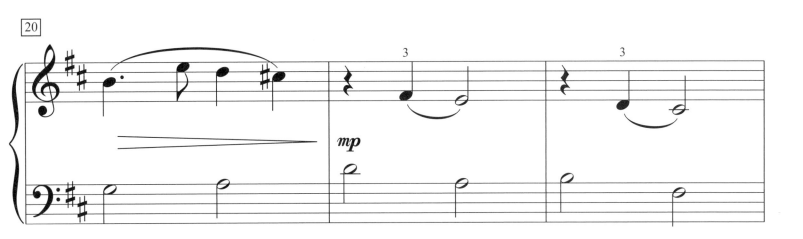

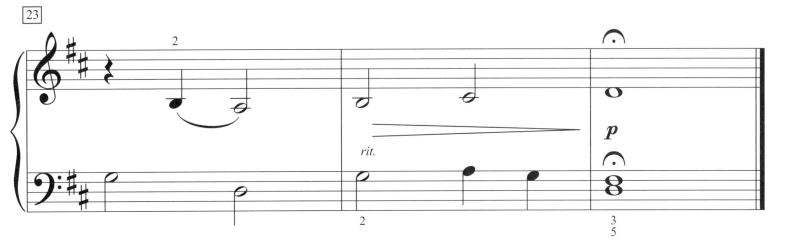

1812 OVERTURE

By PYOTR IL'YICH TCHAIKOVSKY
Arranged by Phillip Keveren

Allegro vivace (♩ = 120)

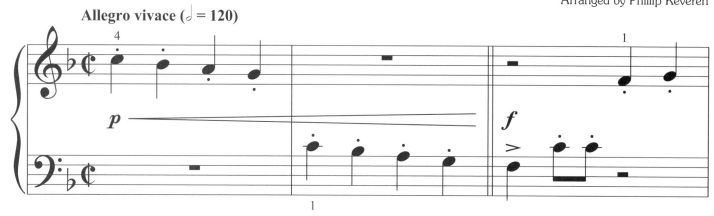

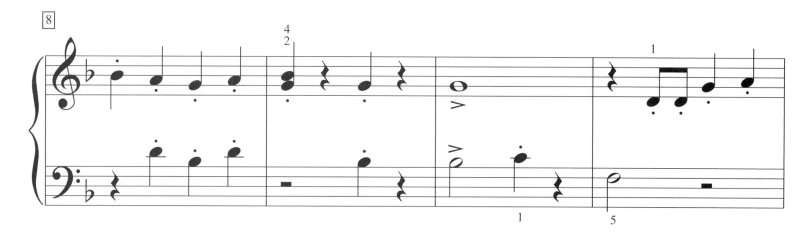

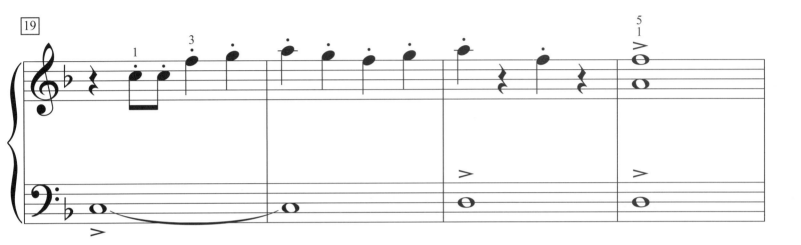

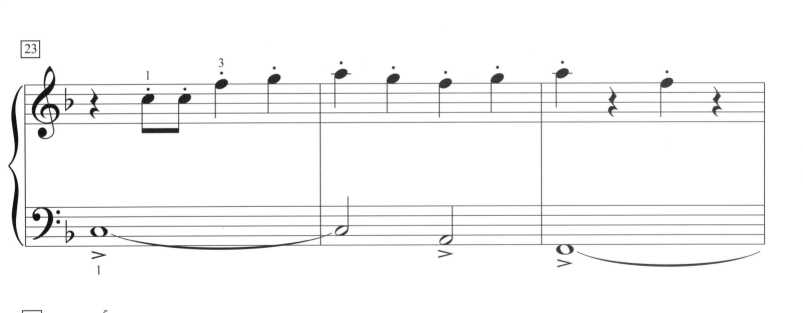

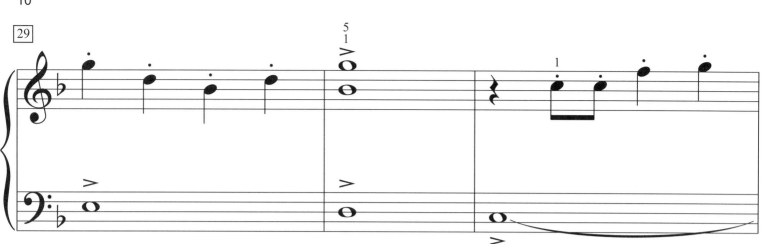

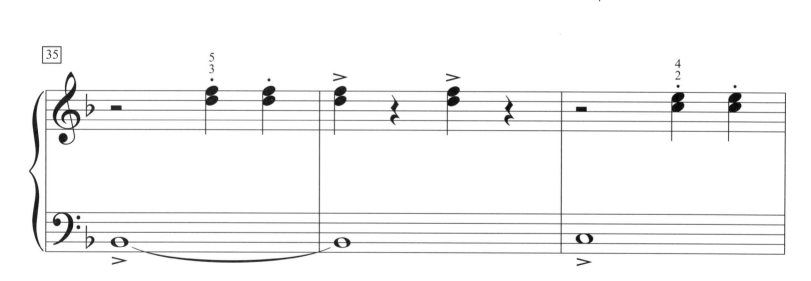

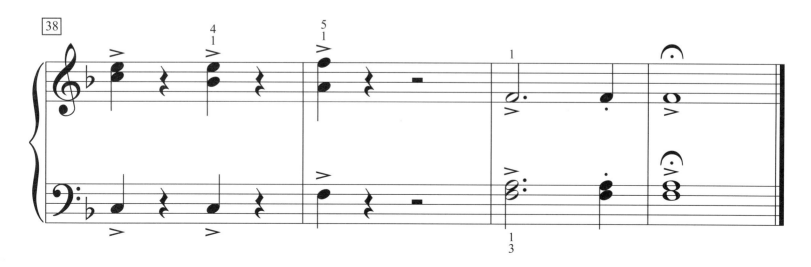

EINE KLEINE NACHTMUSIK
(A Little Night Music)

By WOLFGANG AMADEUS MOZART
Arranged by Phillip Keveren

Allegro (♩ = 120)

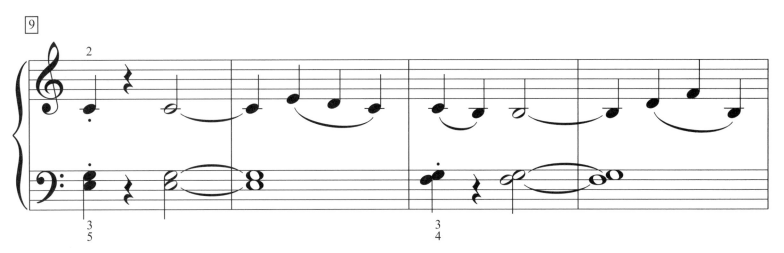

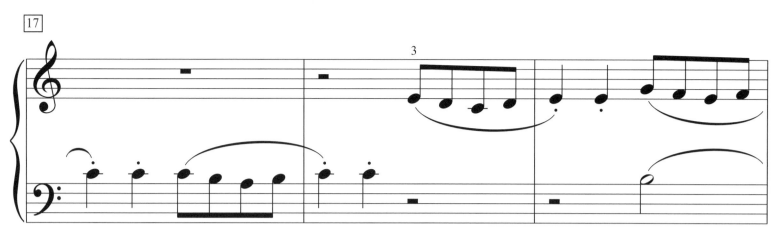

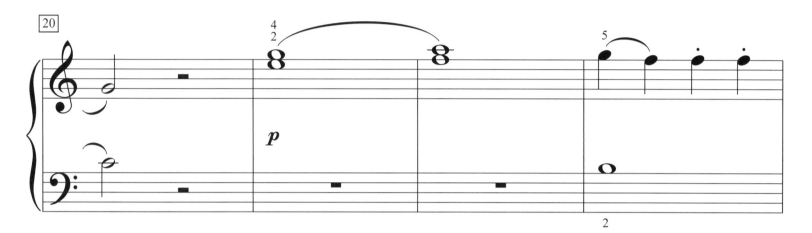

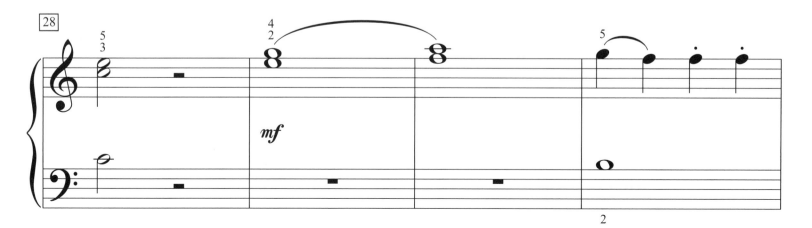

GREAT GATE OF KIEV
from PICTURES AT AN EXHIBITION

By MODEST MUSSORGSKY
Arranged by Phillip Keveren

Maestoso (♩ = 63)

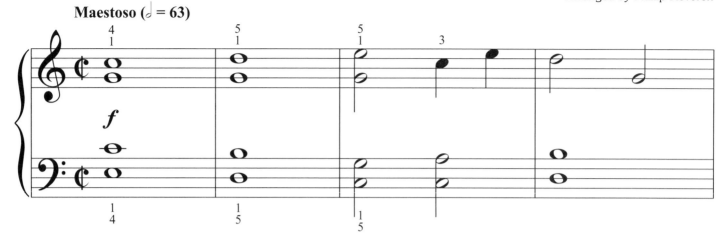

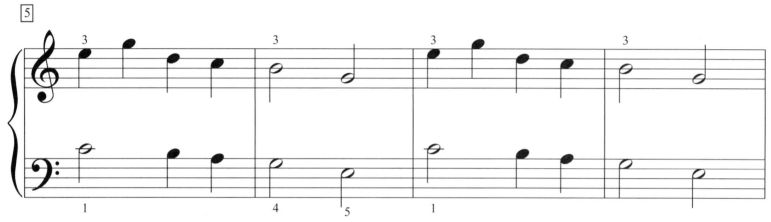

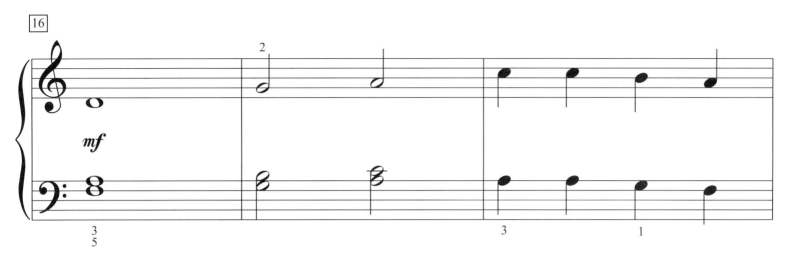

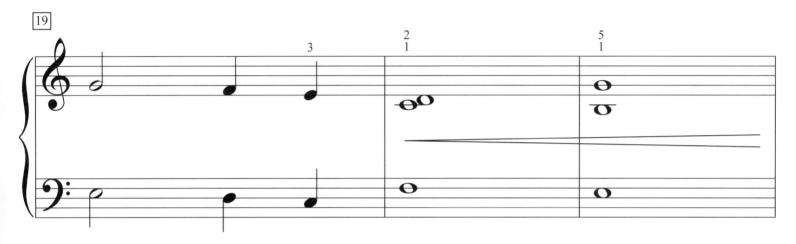

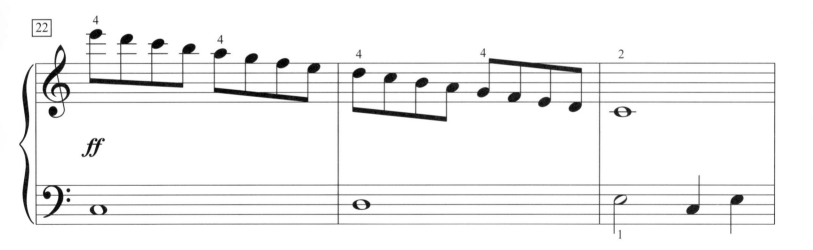

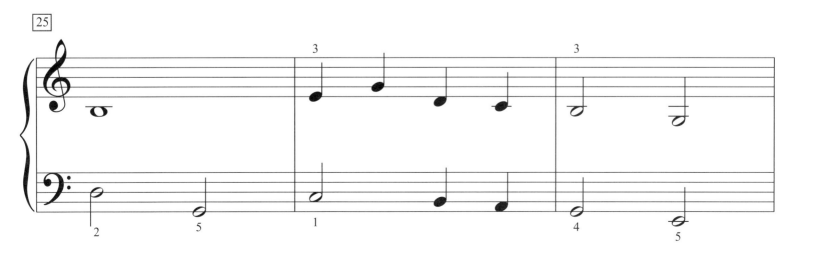

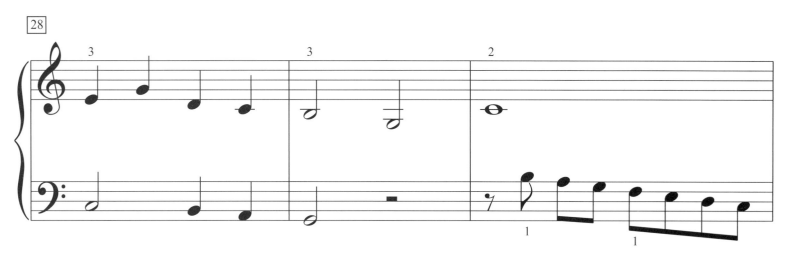

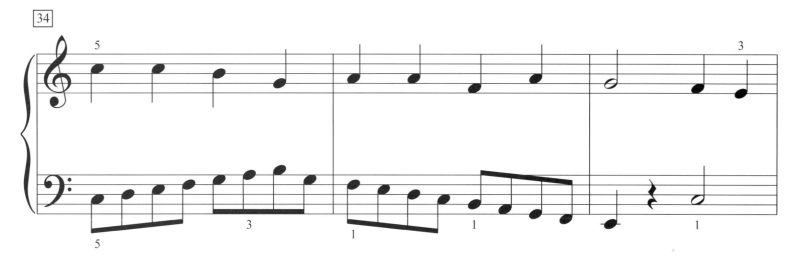

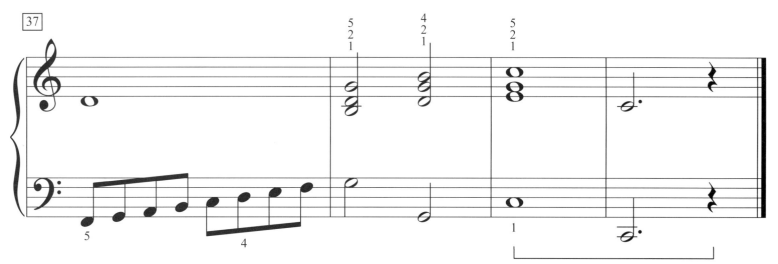

HALLELUJAH CHORUS
from MESSIAH

By GEORGE FRIDERIC HANDEL
Arranged by Phillip Keveren

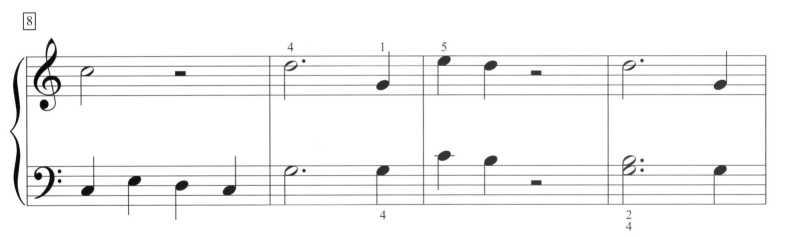

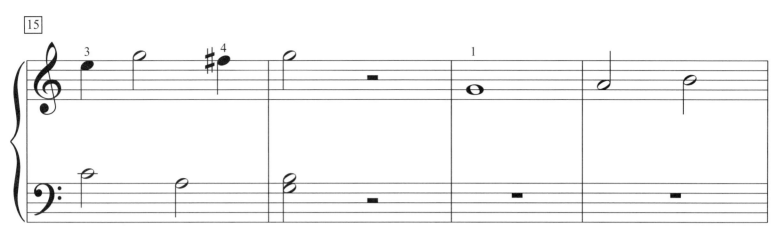

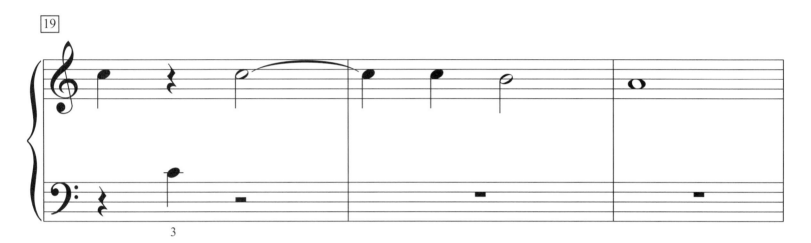

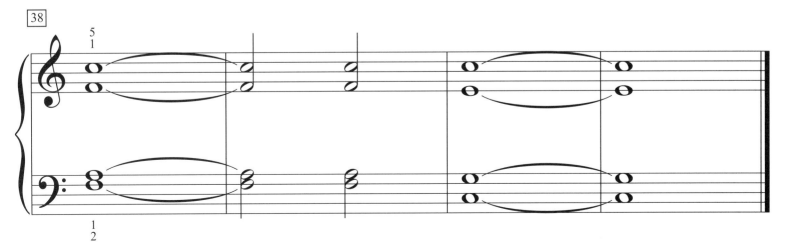

IN THE HALL
OF THE MOUNTAIN KING

from PEER GYNT

By EDVARD GRIEG
Arranged by Phillip Keveren

March (♩ = 104)

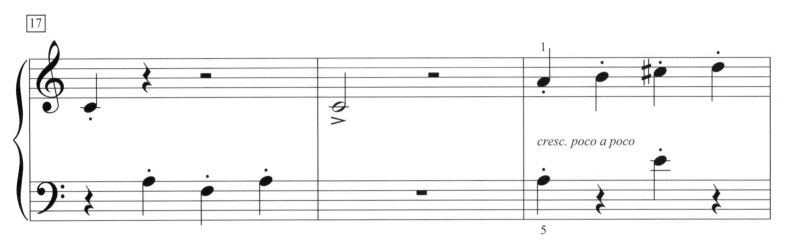

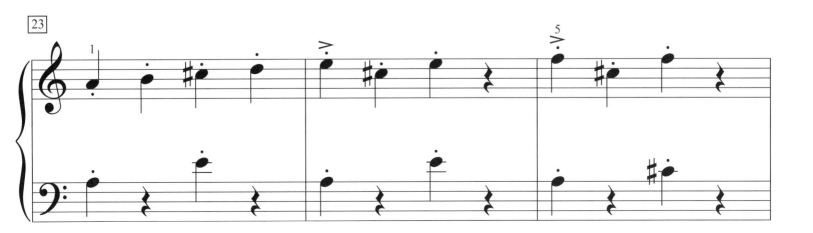

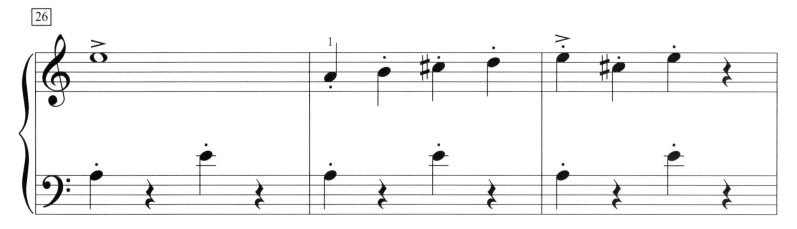

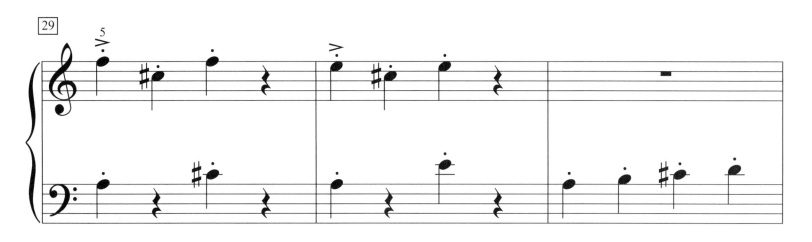

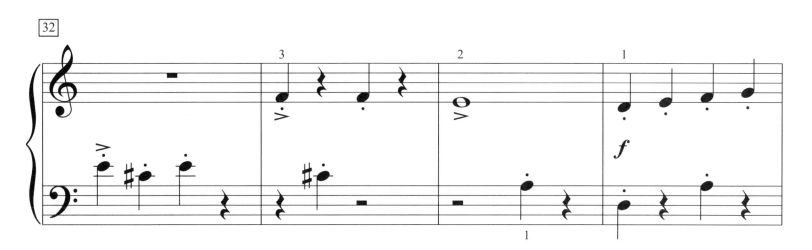

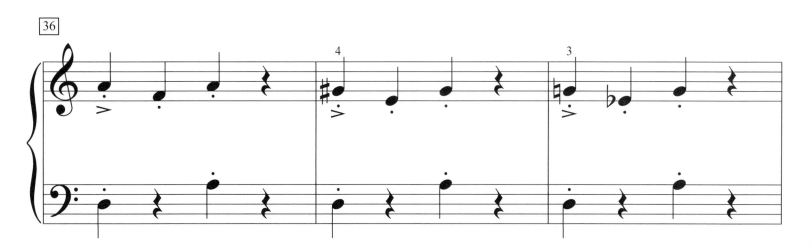

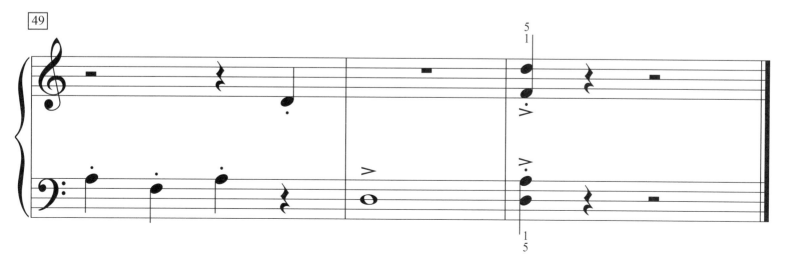

JESU, JOY OF MAN'S DESIRING

from Cantata No. 147

By JOHANN SEBASTIAN BACH
Arranged by Phillip Keveren

Flowing gracefully (♩. = 60)

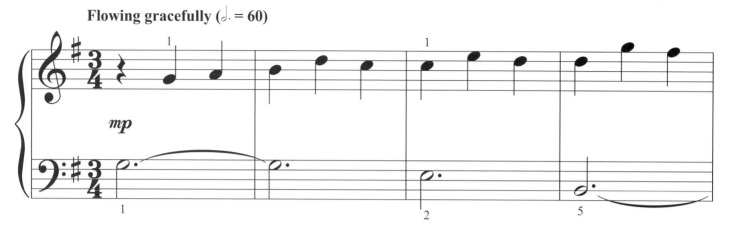

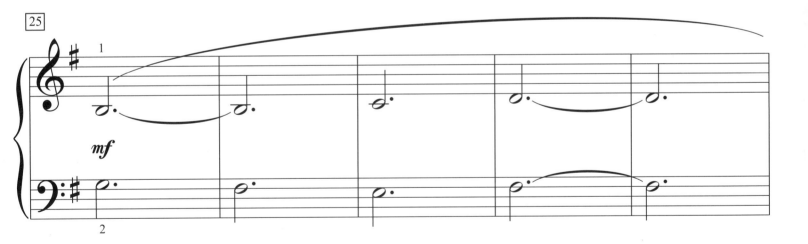

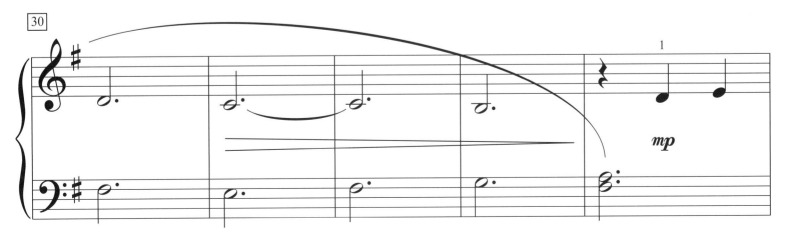

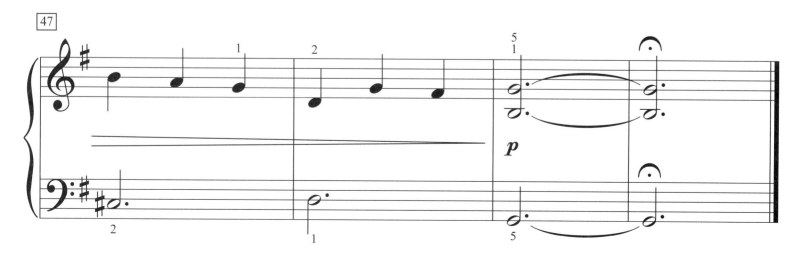

PANIS ANGELICUS
(O Lord Most Holy)

By CÉSAR FRANCK
Arranged by Phillip Keveren

Poco lento (♩ = 72)

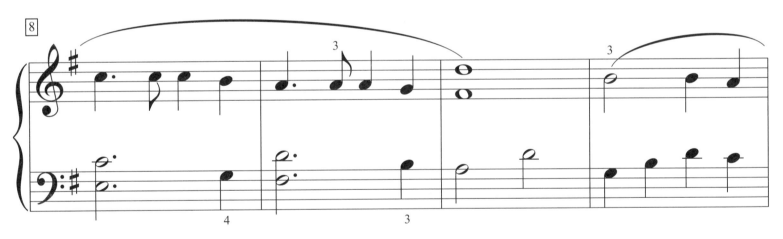

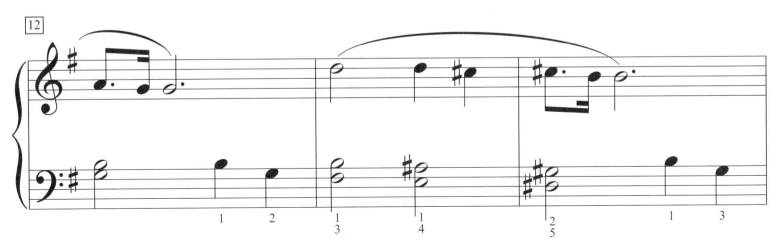

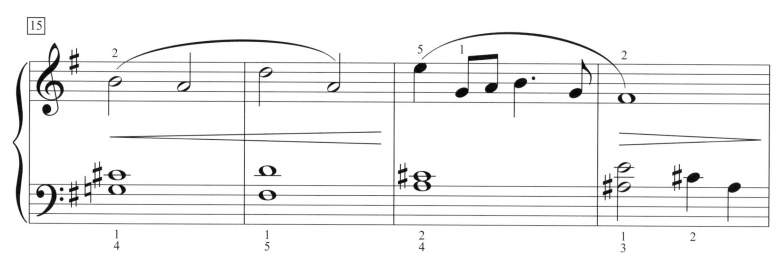

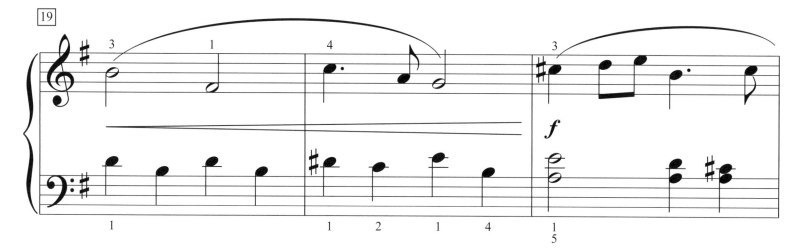

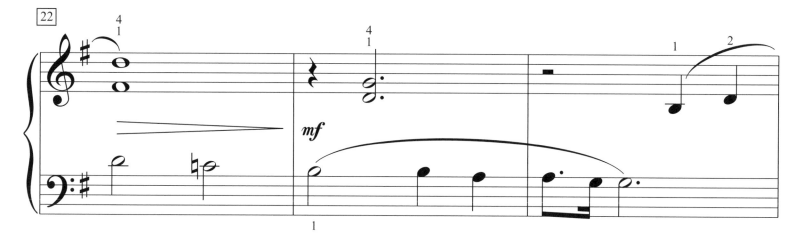

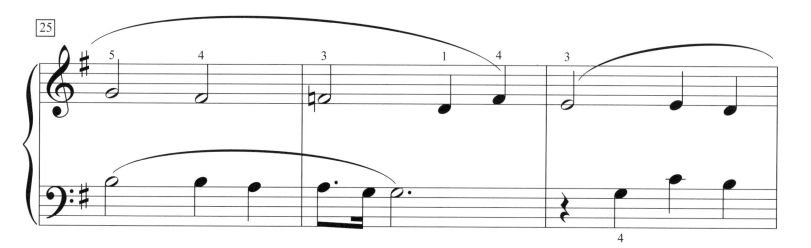

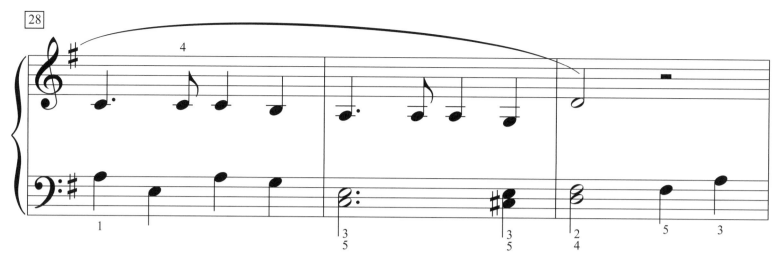

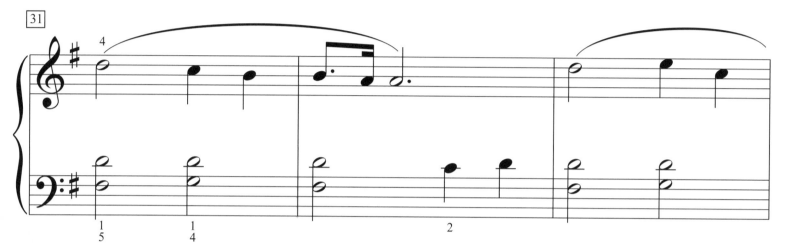

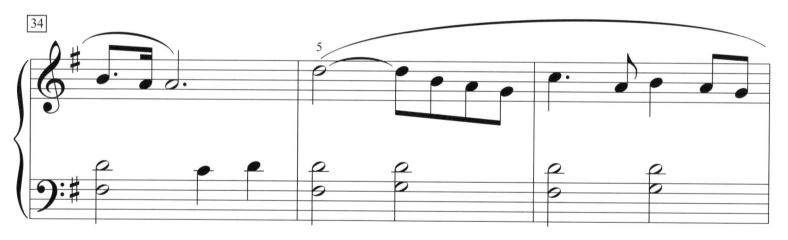

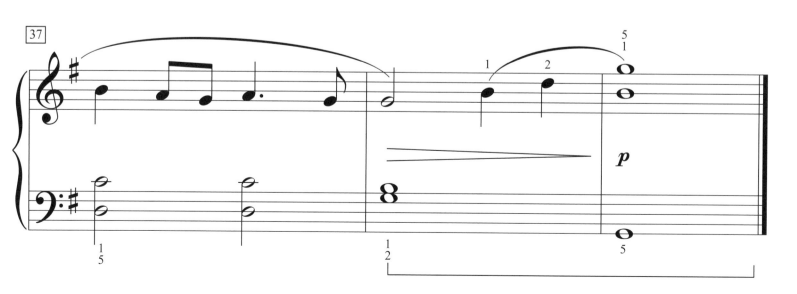

PIANO CONCERTO NO. 1

By PYOTR IL'YICH TCHAIKOVSKY
Arranged by Phillip Keveren

Andante maestoso (♩ = 92)

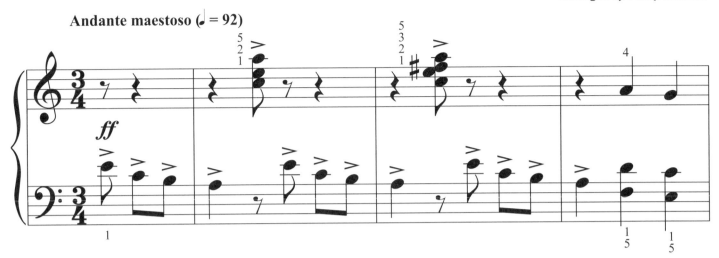

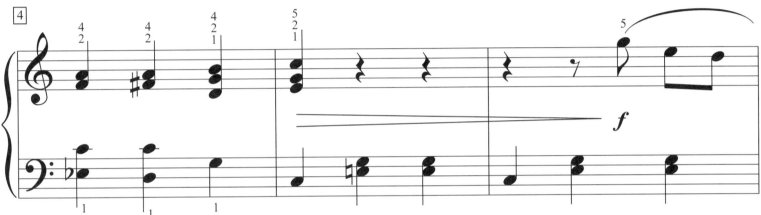

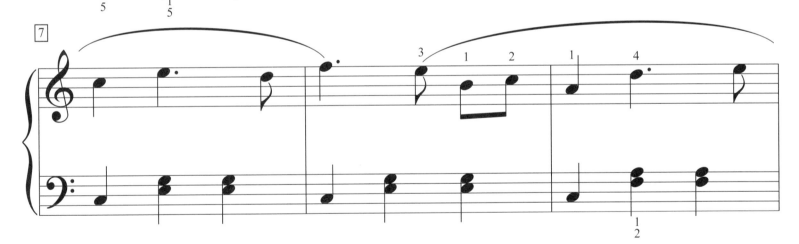

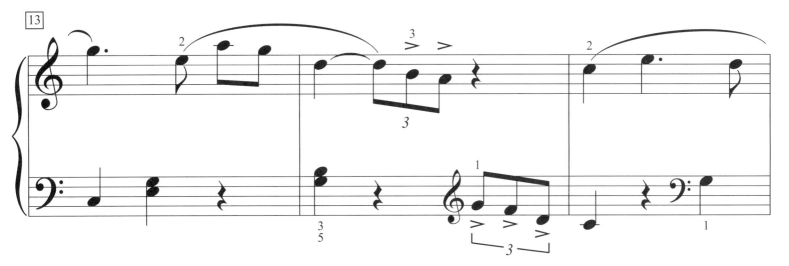

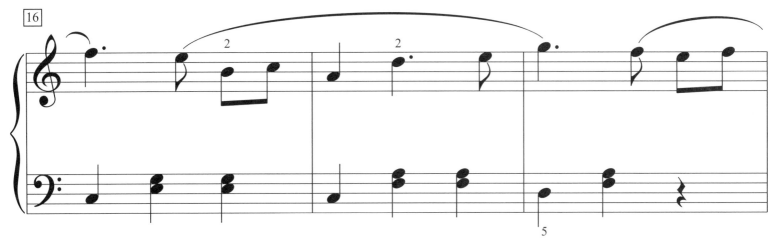

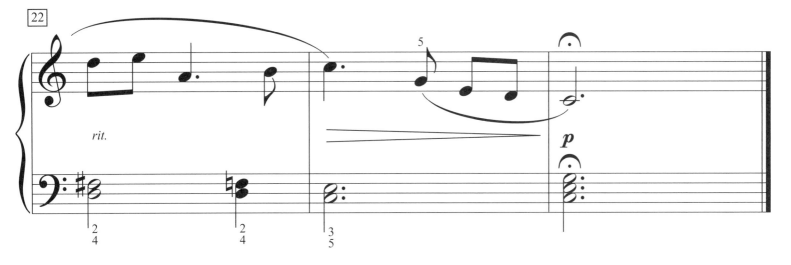

POLOVETSIAN DANCES
from PRINCE IGOR

By ALEXANDER BORODIN
Arranged by Phillip Keveren

Andantino ($\quad$ = 116)

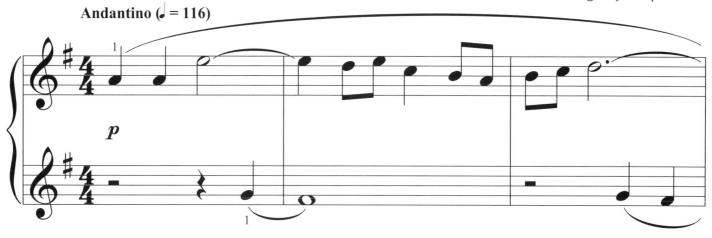

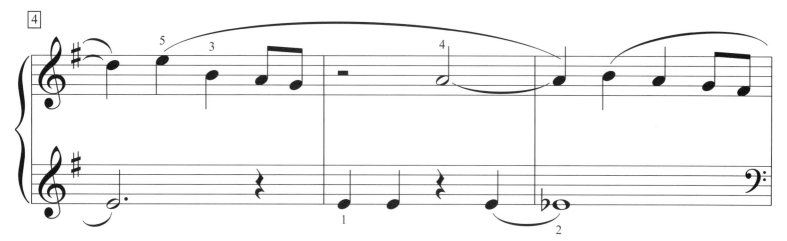

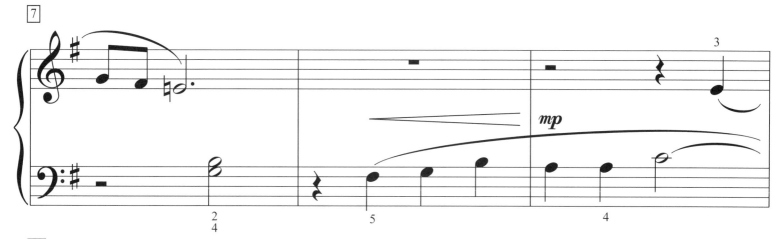

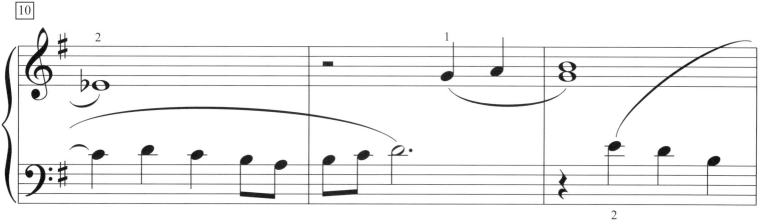

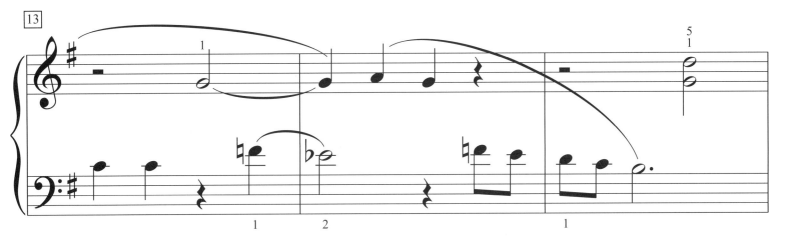

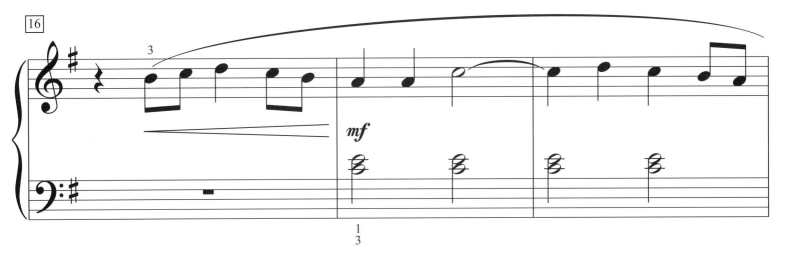

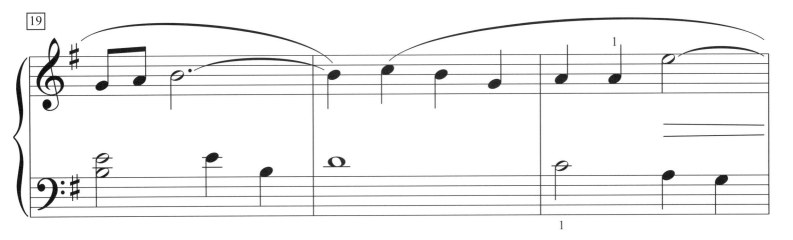

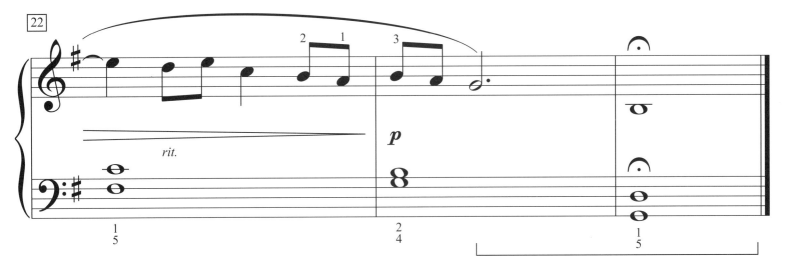

SALUT D'AMOUR
(Greeting to Love)

By EDWARD ELGAR
Arranged by Phillip Keveren

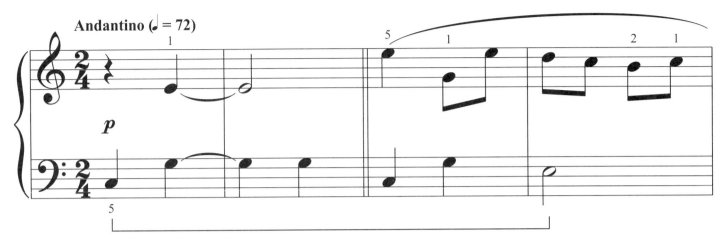

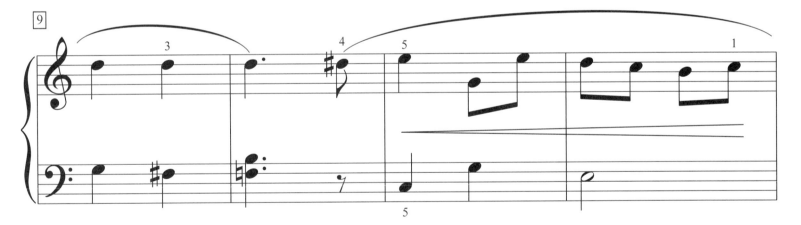

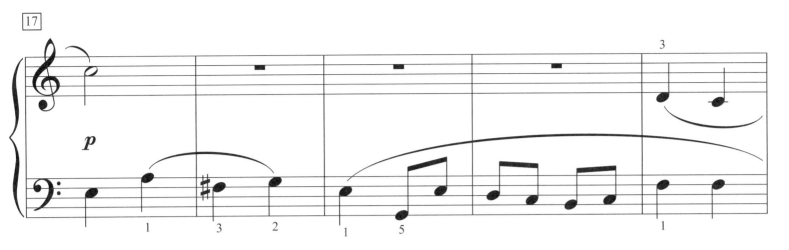

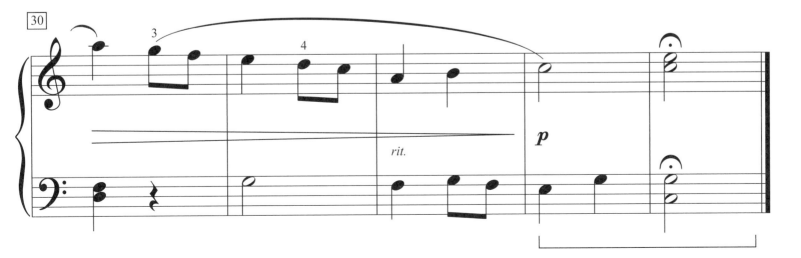

TOCCATA AND FUGUE IN D MINOR

By JOHANN SEBASTIAN BACH
Arranged by Phillip Keveren

Adagio (♩ = c. 80)

TOCCATA

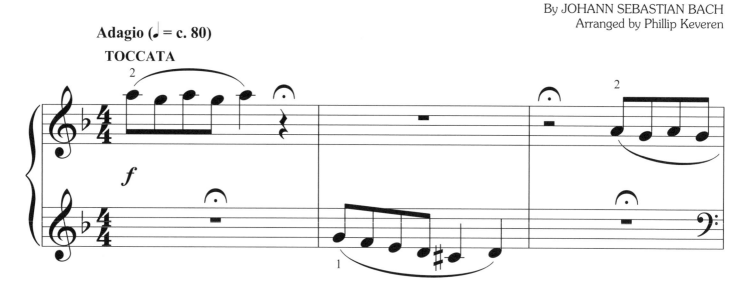

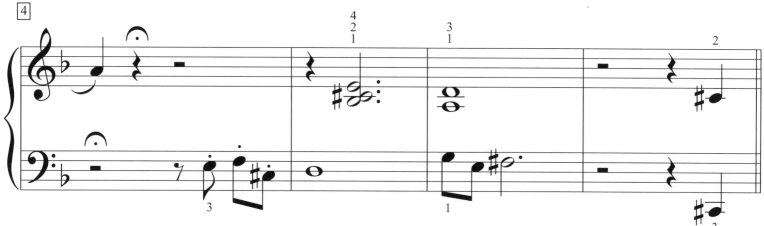

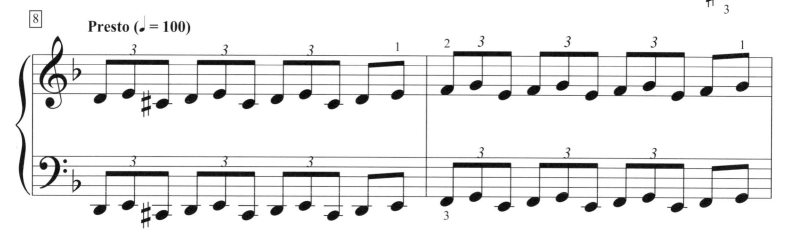

Presto (♩ = 100)

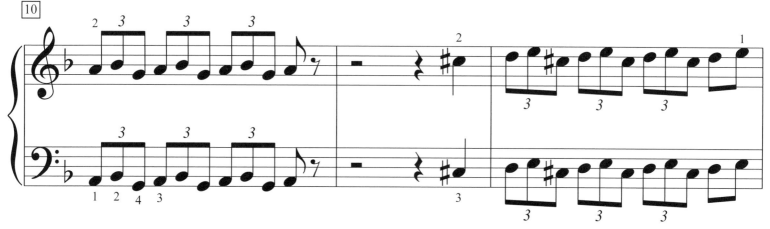

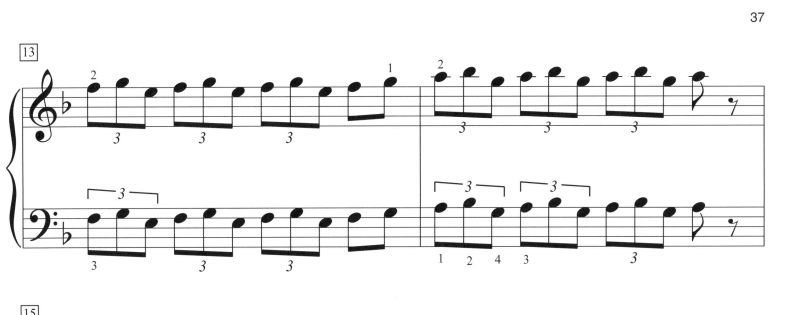

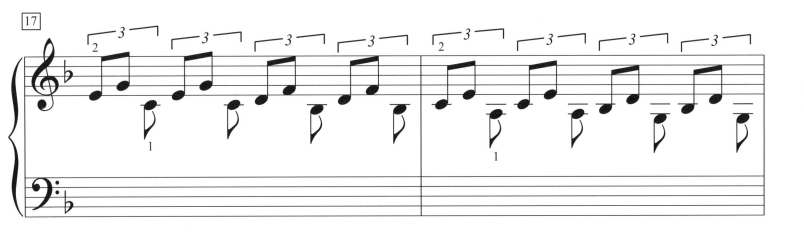

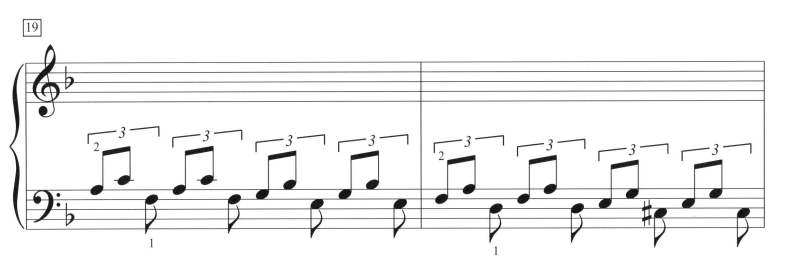

Allegro (♩ = 132)
FUGUE

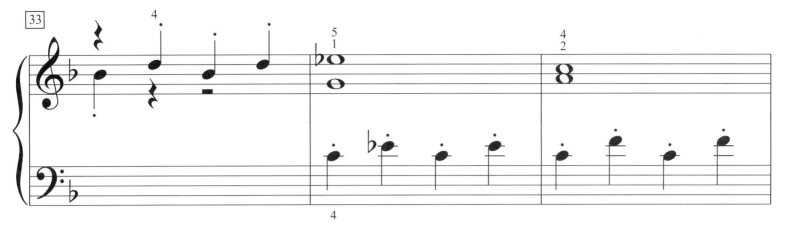

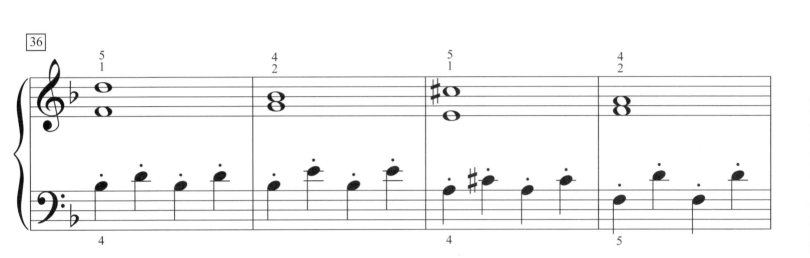

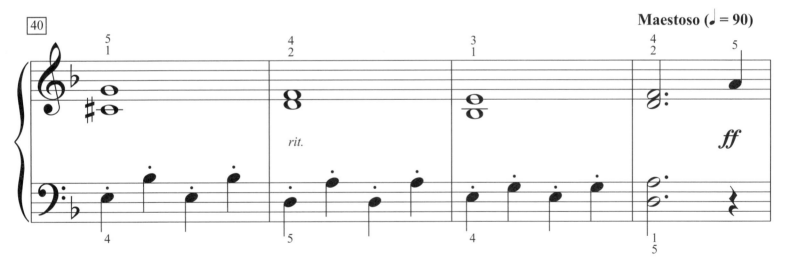

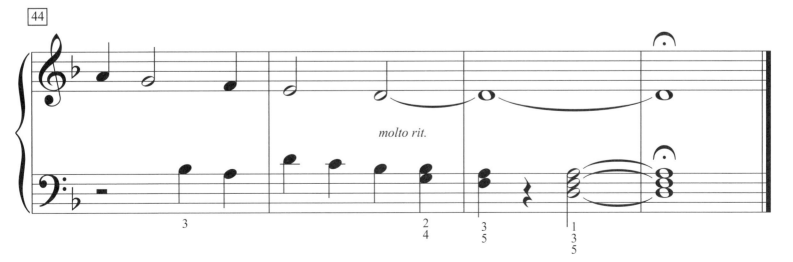

WILLIAM TELL OVERTURE

By GIOACHINO ROSSINI
Arranged by Phillip Keveren

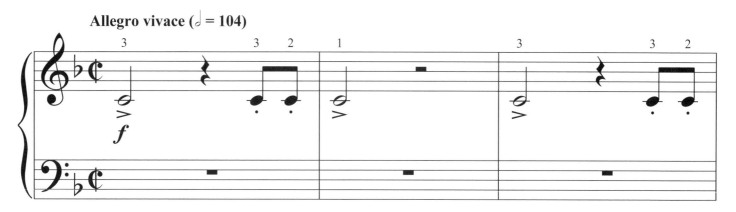

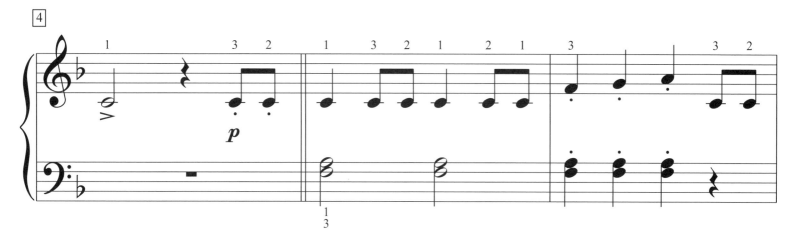

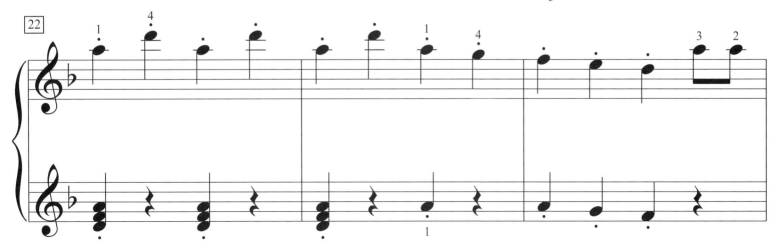

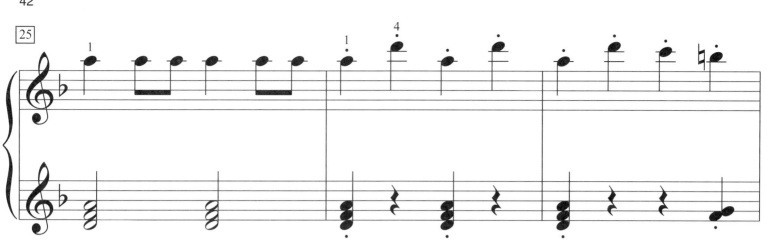

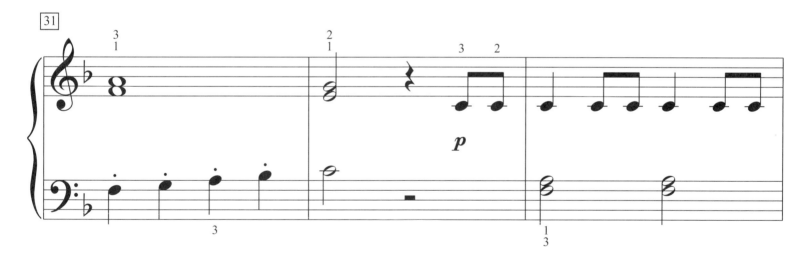

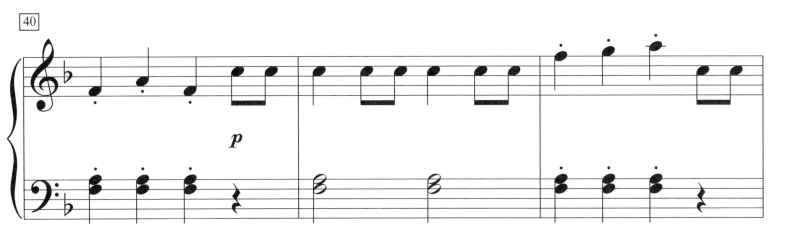

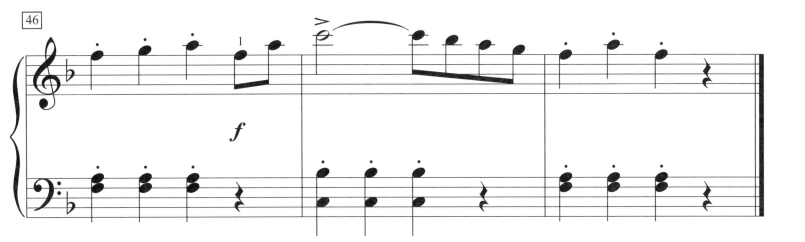

SYMPHONY NO. 5 IN C MINOR
First Movement Excerpt

By LUDWIG VAN BEETHOVEN
Arranged by Phillip Keveren

Allegro con brio (♩ = 100)

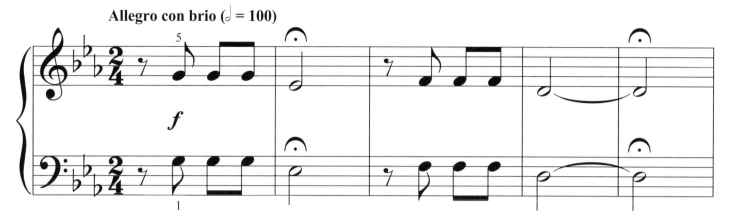

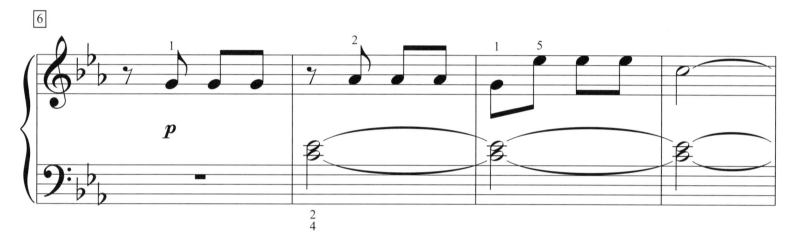

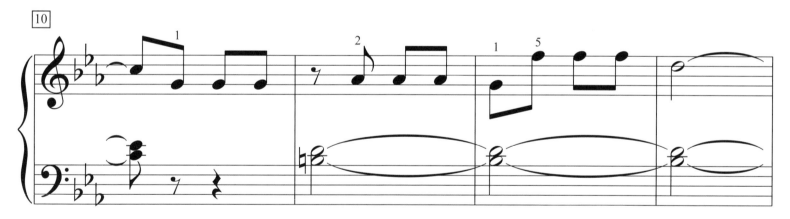

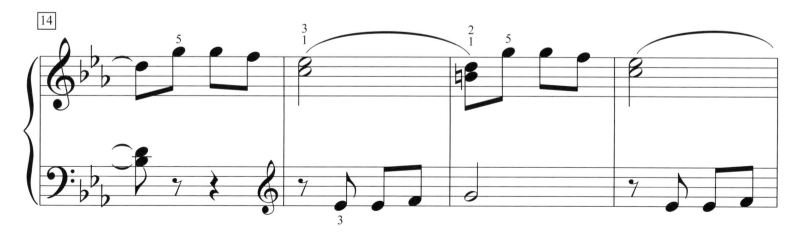

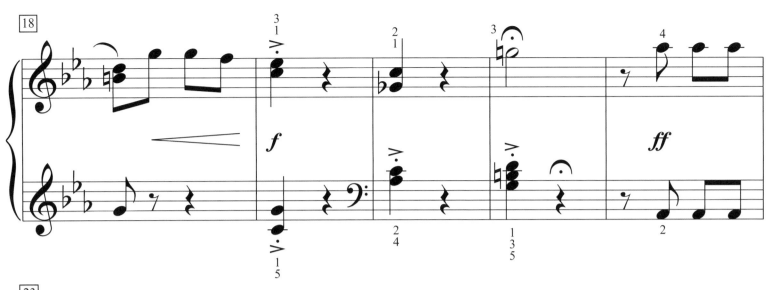

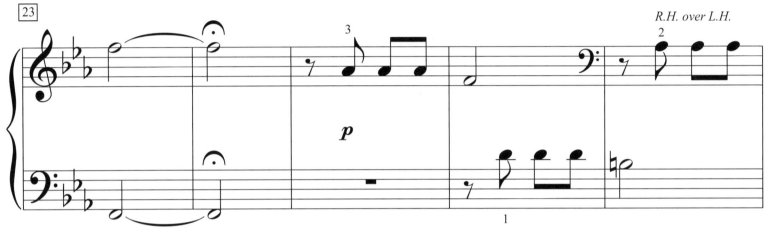

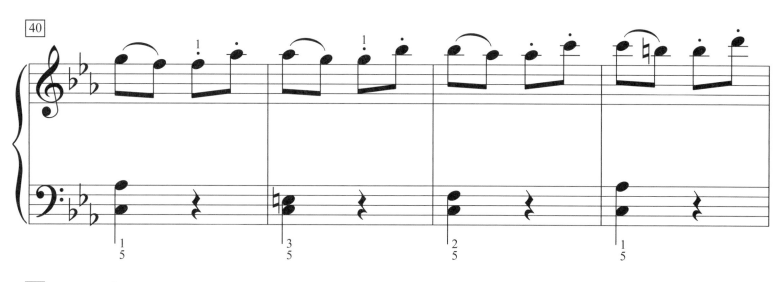

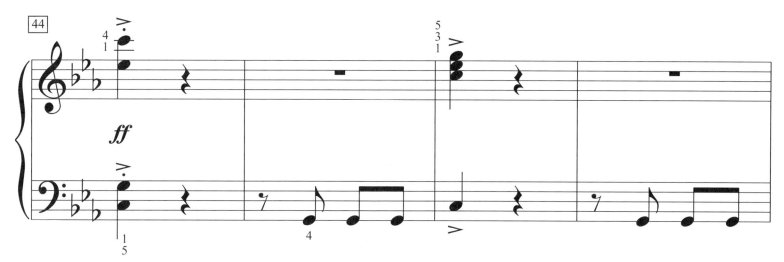

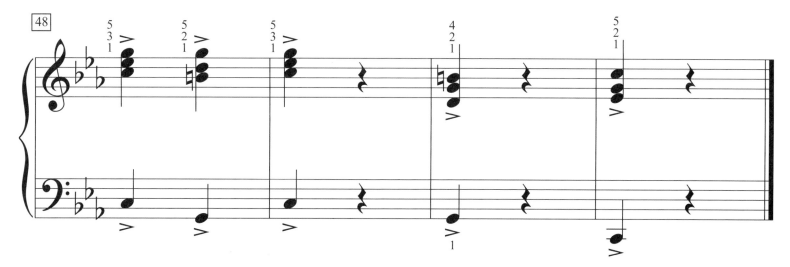

THE PHILLIP KEVEREN SERIES

PIANO SOLO

ABBA FOR CLASSICAL PIANO
00156644...$14.99

ABOVE ALL
00311024...$12.99

BACH MEETS JAZZ
00198473...$14.99

THE BEATLES
00306412...$16.99

THE BEATLES FOR CLASSICAL PIANO
00312189...$14.99

BEST PIANO SOLOS
00312546...$14.99

BLESSINGS
00156601...$12.99

BLUES CLASSICS
00198656...$12.99

BROADWAY'S BEST
00310669...$14.99

A CELTIC CHRISTMAS
00310629...$12.99

THE CELTIC COLLECTION
00310549...$12.95

CHRISTMAS PRAISE HYMNS
00236669...$12.99

CHRISTMAS MEDLEYS
00311414...$12.99

CHRISTMAS AT THE MOVIES
00312190...$14.99

CHRISTMAS SONGS FOR CLASSICAL PIANO
00233788...$12.99

CHRISTMAS WORSHIP MEDLEYS
00311769...$12.99

CINEMA CLASSICS
00310607...$14.99

CLASSICAL JAZZ
00311083...$12.95

COLDPLAY FOR CLASSICAL PIANO
00137779...$14.99

CONTEMPORARY WEDDING SONGS
00311103...$12.99

DISNEY RECITAL SUITES
00249097...$16.99

DISNEY SONGS FOR CLASSICAL PIANO
00311754...$16.99

DISNEY SONGS FOR RAGTIME PIANO
00241379...$16.99

THE FILM SCORE COLLECTION
00311811...$14.99

GOLDEN SCORES
00233789...$14.99

GOSPEL GREATS
00144351...$12.99

THE GREAT AMERICAN SONGBOOK
00183566...$12.99

GREAT STANDARDS
00311157...$12.95

THE HYMN COLLECTION
00311071...$12.99

HYMN MEDLEYS
00311349...$12.99

HYMNS WITH A TOUCH OF JAZZ
00311249...$12.99

I COULD SING OF YOUR LOVE FOREVER
00310905...$12.95

JINGLE JAZZ
00310762...$14.99

BILLY JOEL FOR CLASSICAL PIANO
00175310...$14.99

ELTON JOHN FOR CLASSICAL PIANO
00126449...$14.99

LET FREEDOM RING!
00310839...$9.95

ANDREW LLOYD WEBBER
00313227...$15.99

MANCINI MAGIC
00313523...$14.99

MORE DISNEY SONGS FOR CLASSICAL PIANO
00312113...$15.99

MOTOWN HITS
00311295...$12.95

PIAZZOLLA TANGOS
00306870...$15.99

QUEEN FOR CLASSICAL PIANO
00156645...$15.99

RICHARD RODGERS CLASSICS
00310755...$12.95

SHOUT TO THE LORD!
00310699...$12.95

SONGS FROM CHILDHOOD FOR EASY CLASSICAL PIANO
00233688...$12.99

THE SOUND OF MUSIC
00119403...$14.99

SYMPHONIC HYMNS FOR PIANO
00224738...$14.99

TREASURED HYMNS FOR CLASSICAL PIANO
00312112...$14.99

THE TWELVE KEYS OF CHRISTMAS
00144926...$12.99

WORSHIP WITH A TOUCH OF JAZZ
00294036...$12.99

YULETIDE JAZZ
00311911...$17.99

EASY PIANO

AFRICAN-AMERICAN SPIRITUALS
00310610...$10.99

CATCHY SONGS FOR PIANO
00218387...$12.99

CELTIC DREAMS
00310973...$10.95

CHRISTMAS CAROLS FOR EASY CLASSICAL PIANO
00233686...$12.99

CHRISTMAS POPS
00311126...$14.99

CLASSIC POP/ROCK HITS
00311548...$12.95

A CLASSICAL CHRISTMAS
00310769...$10.95

CLASSICAL MOVIE THEMES
00310975...$12.99

CONTEMPORARY WORSHIP FAVORITES
00311805...$14.99

DISNEY SONGS FOR EASY CLASSICAL PIANO
00144352...$12.99

EARLY ROCK 'N' ROLL
00311093...$10.99

EASY WORSHIP MEDLEYS
00311997...$12.99

FOLKSONGS FOR EASY CLASSICAL PIANO
00160297...$12.99

GEORGE GERSHWIN CLASSICS
00110374...$12.99

GOSPEL TREASURES
00310805...$12.99

THE VINCE GUARALDI COLLECTION
00306821...$16.99

HYMNS FOR EASY CLASSICAL PIANO
00160294...$12.99

IMMORTAL HYMNS
00310798...$10.95

JAZZ STANDARDS
00311294...$12.99

LOVE SONGS
00310744...$10.95

THE MOST BEAUTIFUL SONGS FOR EASY CLASSICAL PIANO
00233740...$12.99

POP STANDARDS FOR EASY CLASSICAL PIANO
00233739...$12.99

RAGTIME CLASSICS
00311293...$10.95

SONGS OF INSPIRATION
00103258...$12.99

SWEET LAND OF LIBERTY
00310840...$10.99

TIMELESS PRAISE
00310712...$12.95

10,000 REASONS
00126450...$14.99

TV THEMES
00311086...$12.99

21 GREAT CLASSICS
00310717...$12.99

WEEKLY WORSHIP
00145342...$16.99

BIG-NOTE PIANO

CHILDREN'S FAVORITE MOVIE SONGS
00310838...$12.99

CHRISTMAS MUSIC
00311247...$10.95

CONTEMPORARY HITS
00310907...$12.99

HOW GREAT IS OUR GOD
00311402...$12.95

INTERNATIONAL FOLKSONGS
00311830...$12.99

JOY TO THE WORLD
00310888...$10.95

THE NUTCRACKER
00310908...$10.99

BEGINNING PIANO SOLOS

AWESOME GOD
00311202...$12.99

CHRISTIAN CHILDREN'S FAVORITES
00310837...$12.99

CHRISTMAS FAVORITES
00311246...$10.95

CHRISTMAS TIME IS HERE
00311334...$12.99

CHRISTMAS TRADITIONS
00311117...$10.99

EASY HYMNS
00311250...$12.99

KIDS' FAVORITES
00310822...$12.99

PIANO DUET

CLASSICAL THEME DUETS
00311350...$10.99

HYMN DUETS
00311544...$12.99

PRAISE & WORSHIP DUETS
00311203...$11.95

STAR WARS
00119405...$14.99

WORSHIP SONGS FOR TWO
00253545...$12.99

Big Fun with Big-Note Piano Books!

These songbooks feature exciting easy arrangements for beginning piano students.

Best of Adele

Now even beginners can play their favorite Adele tunes! This book features big-note arrangements of 10 top songs: Chasing Pavements • Daydreamer • Hometown Glory • Lovesong • Make You Feel My Love • One and Only • Rolling in the Deep • Set Fire to the Rain • Someone like You • Turning Tables.
00308601 ....$12.99

Beatles' Best

27 classics for beginners to enjoy, including: Can't Buy Me Love • Eleanor Rigby • Hey Jude • Michelle • Here, There and Everywhere • When I'm Sixty-Four • Yesterday • and more.
00222561....................................$14.99

The Best Songs Ever

70 favorites, featuring: Body and Soul • Crazy • Edelweiss • Fly Me to the Moon • Georgia on My Mind • Imagine • The Lady Is a Tramp • Memory • A String of Pearls • Tears in Heaven • Unforgettable • You Are So Beautiful • and more.
00310425 ....$19.95

Children's Favorite Movie Songs

arranged by Phillip Keveren
16 favorites from films, including: The Bare Necessities • Beauty and the Beast • Can You Feel the Love Tonight • Do-Re-Mi • The Rainbow Connection • Tomorrow • Zip-A-Dee-Doo-Dah • and more.
00310838 ....$12.99

Classical Music's Greatest Hits

24 beloved classical pieces, including: Air on the G String • Ave Maria • By the Beautiful Blue Danube • Canon in D • Eine Kleine Nachtmusik • Für Elise • Ode to Joy • Romeo and Juliet • Waltz of the Flowers • more.
00310475 ....$12.99

Disney Big-Note Collection

Over 40 Disney favorites, including: Circle of Life • Colors of the Wind • Hakuna Matata • It's a Small World • Under the Sea • A Whole New World • Winnie the Pooh • Zip-A-Dee-Doo-Dah • and more.
00316056..$19.99

Essential Classical

22 simplified piano pieces from top composers, including: Ave Maria (Schubert) • Blue Danube Waltz (Strauss) • Für Elise (Beethoven) • Jesu, Joy of Man's Desiring (Bach) • Morning (Grieg) • Pomp and Circumstance (Elgar) • and many more.
00311205..$10.99

Favorite Children's Songs

arranged by Bill Boyd
29 easy arrangements of songs to play and sing with children: Peter Cottontail • I Whistle a Happy Tune • It's a Small World • On the Good Ship Lollipop • The Rainbow Connection • and more!
00240251..$10.95

Frozen

9 songs from this hit Disney film, plus full-color illustrations from the movie. Songs include the standout single "Let It Go", plus: Do You Want to Build a Snowman? • For the First Time in Forever • Reindeer(s) Are Better Than People • and more.
00126105 ....$12.99

Happy Birthday to You and Other Great Songs for Big-Note Piano

16 essential favorites, including: Chitty Chitty Bang Bang • Good Night • Happy Birthday to You • Heart and Soul • Over the Rainbow • Sing • This Land Is Your Land • and more.
00119636 ....$9.99

Elton John – Greatest Hits

20 of his biggest hits, including: Bennie and the Jets • Candle in the Wind • Crocodile Rock • Rocket Man • Tiny Dancer • Your Song • and more.
00221832..$12.99

Les Misérables

14 favorites from the Broadway sensation arranged for beginning pianists. Titles include: At the End of the Day • Bring Him Home • Castle on a Cloud • I Dreamed a Dream • In My Life • On My Own • Who Am I? • and more.
00221812 ....$14.95

The Phantom of the Opera

9 songs from the Broadway spectacular, including: All I Ask of You • Angel of Music • Masquerade • The Music of the Night • The Phantom of the Opera • The Point of No Return • Prima Donna • Think of Me • Wishing You Were Somehow Here Again.
00110006 ....$14.99

Pride & Prejudice
Music from the Motion Picture Soundtrack

12 piano pieces from the 2006 Oscar-nominated film: Another Dance • Darcy's Letter • Georgiana • Leaving Netherfield • Liz on Top of the World • Meryton Townhall • The Secret Life of Daydreams • Stars and Butterflies • and more.
00316125 ....$12.99

The Sound of Music

arranged by Phillip Keveren
9 favorites: Climb Ev'ry Mountain • Do-Re-Mi • Edelweiss • The Lonely Goatherd • Maria • My Favorite Things • Sixteen Going on Seventeen • So Long, Farewell • The Sound of Music.
00316057..$10.99

Best of Taylor Swift

A dozen top tunes from this crossover sensation: Fearless • Fifteen • Hey Stephen • Love Story • Our Song • Picture to Burn • Teardrops on My Guitar • White Horse • You Belong with Me • and more.
00307143 ....$12.99

Worship Favorites

20 powerful songs: Above All • Come, Now Is the Time to Worship • I Could Sing of Your Love Forever • More Precious Than Silver • Open the Eyes of My Heart • Shout to the Lord • and more.
00311207..$10.95

Complete song lists online at
www.halleonard.com

0318